HORSEPOWER

SNOWMOBILES

by Matt Doeden

Reading Consultant:

Barbara J. Fox

Reading Specialist

North Carolina State University

Capstone
press

Mankato, Minnesota

Blazers is published by Capstone Press,
151 Good Counsel Drive, P.O. Box 669, Mankato, Minnesota 56002.
www.capstonepress.com

Library of Congress Cataloging-in-Publication Data
Doeden, Matt.
    Snowmobiles / by Matt Doeden.
        p. cm.—(Blazers. Horsepower)
    Includes bibliographical references and index.
    ISBN 0-7368-3791-4 (hardcover)
    ISBN 0-7368-5214-X (paperback)
        1. Snowmobiling—Juvenile literature. I. Title. II. Series.
GV856.5.D64 2005
796.94—dc22   2004018880

Summary: Discusses snowmobiles, their main features, and how
    they are raced.

Editorial Credits
Erika L. Shores, editor; Jason Knudson, set designer; Patrick D.
    Dentinger, book designer; Wanda Winch, photo researcher;
    Scott Thoms, photo editor

Photo Credits
Corbis/Duomo/Chris Trotman, cover
Getty Images Inc./Brian Bahr, 4–5, 7, 8–9, 25; Donald Miralle, 6,
    16–17, 24
Linda Aksomitis, 12–13, 14–15, 19, 20–21, 22–23, 26–27, 28–29
Tomasoski Photography, 10–11, 18

1 2 3 4 5 6 10 09 08 07 06 05

TABLE OF CONTENTS

THE RACE

Six snowmobiles take off from the starting line. Their engines whine as they race toward the first turn.

The snowmobiles sail over a jump.
A black snowmobile bursts into the
lead. Soon a green snowmobile tries
to pass.

BLAZER FACT

In 1968, a group of explorers used snowmobiles to reach the North Pole.

The snowmobiles speed around the final turn. They fly over a jump, then cross the finish line. The green snowmobile wins by inches.

SNOWMOBILE DESIGN

The frame is the main body of a snowmobile. A snowmobile needs a strong frame to land from high jumps.

The engine turns wheels that move a track. The track has sharp bumps to grip snow and ice.

Wheel

Track

Riders use handlebars to turn the skis. The skis slide over the snow.

BLAZER FACT

Polaris, Arctic Cat, Ski-Doo, and Yamaha make most snowmobiles.

Handlebars

Skis

SPEEDING THROUGH SNOW

The fastest snowmobiles can go more than 100 miles (160 kilometers) per hour.

Riders use a throttle to control speed. To go faster, riders press a trigger on the handlebars.

BLAZER FACT

The fastest measured snowmobile speed was 167 miles (269 kilometers) per hour.

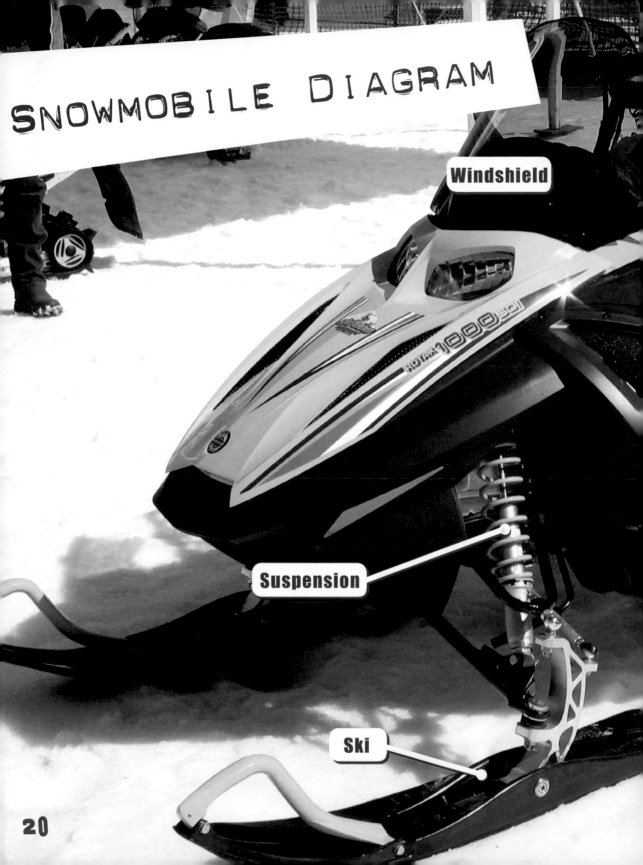

SNOWMOBILE DIAGRAM

Windshield

Suspension

Ski

Handlebars

Track

Wheel

SNOWMOBILES IN ACTION

The most daring riders drive in snocross races. They race around sharp turns. They fly over hills and jumps.

Snocross courses have big jumps. Racers sail over jumps and launch their snowmobiles into the air.

Safety is important to snowmobile riders. They wear gloves and warm clothes. Helmets protect their heads during crashes.

BLAZER FACT

In watercross races, snowmobile riders race across water.

LEANING INTO A TURN!

GLOSSARY

frame (FRAYM)—the main body of a snowmobile

snocross (SNOH-krawss)—a snowmobile race in which drivers speed around a course with tight turns and jumps

throttle (THROT-uhl)—a lever that controls how much fuel and air flow into an engine; a rider presses the throttle trigger to speed up.

track (TRAK)—a long metal belt that runs around a snowmobile's wheels to grip snow and ice

trigger (TRIG-uhr)—a lever on a snowmobile's handlebars that controls the throttle

READ MORE

Budd, E. S. *Snowmobiles.* Sport Machines at Work. Chanhassen, Minn.: Child's World, 2004.

Dubois, Muriel. *Snowmobiles.* Wild Rides! Mankato, Minn. Capstone Press, 2002.

Mara, William P. *Snowmobile Racing.* Motorsports. Mankato, Minn. Capstone Press, 1999.

INTERNET SITES

FactHound offers a safe, fun way to find Internet sites related to this book. All of the sites on FactHound have been researched by our staff.

Here's how:

1. Visit *www.facthound.com*
2. Type in this special code **0736837914** for age-appropriate sites. Or, enter a search word related to this book for a more general search.
3. Click on the **Fetch It** button.

FactHound will fetch the best sites for you!

INDEX